"Dog lovers, g
book gives tl
strategies to become the pack leader."—
Daily Dog

*"You owe yourself a visit to Rhodes' School
for Dogs, where members range from
Border Collie pups to Great Danes to just
about everything in between."*—The Santa
Monica Courant

*"Rhodes' techniques are rooted in tradition
and in a sense of how positive
reinforcement can serve as a powerful
memory for life."*—Darren Matheny

© Copyright 2018 Antony Rhodes

All rights reserved.

No part of this publication may be reproduced, stored in a
retrieval system, or transmitted, in any form or by any
means, without the prior permission in writing of the
publisher, nor be otherwise circulated in any form of
binding or cover other than that in which it is published and
without a similar condition including this condition being
imposed on the subsequent purchaser.

Published by Mobius Publishing Limited

Furbo Dog Camera

Treat Tossing, Full HD Wifi Pet Camera and 2-Way Audio, Designed For Dogs, Works With Amazon Alexa (As Seen On Ellen)

- Fun TREAT TOSSING: TOSS a treat to your dogs via the free Furbo iOS/Android app. Fill it with over 100 pieces of your dogs' favorite treats & play a game of catch.

- 1080p Camera & Night Vision: livestream video to monitor your pet with a 160° wide-angle view, day and night.

- 2-Way Chat & BARKING ALERT: Furbo's BARKING SENSOR is MADE FOR DOGS. It sends push notifications to your smartphone when it detects barking. Know what's going on at home and talk to calm them down via the app.

- Comes with a Free Smart Dog Alerts Trial: Know exactly what your dog is doing. Furbo uses DOG RECOGNITION TECHNOLOGY to send you Dog Activity Alert, Person Alert & Dog Selfie Alert

To Get It Now, Visit tiny.cc/mpub/dogs

Bonus: FREE E-Book!

As a special thank you to my readers, I am giving away free copies of *Backyard Chickens: The Ultimate Guide.* Enjoy eggs from your backyard while they're still warm! Reconnect with nature and your food by having your own chickens. It's easier than you think.

To get instant access to this book and more awesome resources, visit the link below:

Tiny.cc/mpub/free-gift-backyard-chickens

As an added bonus, subscribers will be given a chance to get exclusive sneak peaks of upcoming books and a chance to get free copies with no strings attached. Don't worry, we treat your e-mail with the respect it deserves. You won't get any spammy emails!!!

Contents

Part 1

Introduction

Congratulations! If you are reading this, it means that you (probably) own a German Shorthaired Pointer, but even better, it means that you want to train your companion into a good doggy.

Doesn't he look adorable? With the aid of your steady efforts, and this handy guide, you will turn that fresh puppy into this beautiful and obedient companion:

You probably know this already, but I'll take this moment to stress why you should definitely train your German Shorthaired Pointer.

- German Shorthaired Pointers are affectionate and obedient! They are friendly and very enthusiastic, even boisterous at times. A trained Pointer can be very loving and versatile!

- Troublesome pets not only get annoying for you after a time, but they do too for your friends and family, and you don't want anyone to feel annoyed by your furry friend, do you?

- A trained German Shorthaired Pointer becomes very independent, up to the point you no longer need to worry about what he's doing all the time. Coupled with their natural willing behavior and bold attitude, you'll have a disciplined home guardian! On top of that, they're amazing companions as well.

- For every person that values his/her pets and also the cleanliness of the house, a trained doggy is a treasure.

- Your friends and family will envy your flawlessly trained canine, and they will wish their dogs were as cool as yours!

Time to get ready!

German Shorthaired Pointers aren't particularly hard to train, but training a dog isn't something you do overnight. It demands time, effort (treats, a lot of treats) and dedication, so be prepared to spend some (money on treats) quality time with your dog. Trust me, in the long run, you (and your furry friend) will thank it, and both of you will have some great memories to share after the training!

You must be firm, without being harsh or hasty. German Shorthaired Pointers are more intelligent than the average breed, and they're also very obedient; they will respond better to a soft, gentle tutor, than a stout, abusive one. Teach them like you would a little kid: with patience, love, and lots of candies!

With this said, and without preamble, let us get right into the business!

Part 2

Basic Information About the German Shorthaired Pointer

First, a little history. The ancestry of the German Shorthaired Pointers is a bit unclear. Many hold that the Pointer descends from a breed that was known ass the German Bird Dog, which is in turn related to the Old Spanish Pointer, introduced to Germany in the 17th century. However, various German hounds and tracking dogs, the English Pointer, and the Arkwright Pointer are said to be possible contributors to the development of the breed. It may be impossible to determine their ancestry with total precision, but the breed was officially recognized in 1930.

As for toys, go for chew toys! Soft, but durable chew toys are often a good bet, but you should get some squeaky toys too, and rope toys as well; don't underestimate the power of a tight knot of rope: the fibers can do wonder's to your dog's dental health, and you can also play with him! He will love your interaction. Links to all the products mentioned below are at tiny.cc/mpub/dogs.

- I like toys that let me play with my dog, s o I recommend this durable toy (Amazon link at tiny.cc/mpub/dogs).

- And this squeaky toy (Amazon link at tiny.cc/mpub/dogs).

- Regarding rope toys, I love this value pack (Amazon link at tiny.cc/mpub/dogs), it even brings flossing toys to provide a myriad of dental benefits!

Remember to have a solid (and good-looking) collar and leash for your dog, not too tight (you don't want to hurt him) but neither too loose, generally, if you can fit two fingers under the collar, it's alright.

- I find myself constantly adjusting the collar of my dog, so I got this adjustable collar (Amazon link at tiny.cc/mpub/dogs) which I recommend.

- I went for a matching 6-foot leash (Amazon link at tiny.cc/mpub/dogs) because why not!

Regarding space, you should avoid confining a German Shorthaired Pointer to a small apartment, or a small space in general. While they don't want to be running around all the time, nor have any health complications because of it, they will want to stretch their legs every now and then. In any case, as long as you provide your friend with sufficient exercise, you shouldn't have issues!

Maybe this little fella doesn't hurt too much but think about how would it be in the future.

**...And you certainly don't want your friend
tearing your shoes apart, do you?**

Very well, we have covered a few points in
this chapter, so let's end with a short list of
things to have in mind:

- Give him things to do! You can't have
  him sitting all day for an entire week,
  they need to put those muscles to work.

- Structure his routine, he needs to feel
  some sense of order and command in his
  life, but remember to leave him time for
  himself.

- Make him socialize! Only that way your
  doggy will truly become a happy animal.

- Give him chew toys, this is super
  important, your expensive couch and
  your shiny shoes will thank you for it.

- Last but not least... don 't confine them

to enclosed environments.

Part 3

House Training

You probably get the idea behind house-training just by the name, but for the sake of clarifying, here I go:

House training can be defined as the training that instills the basic household rules to your furry companion. Especially the ones regarding excretions.

You'll get it right someday!

One thing to have in mind with your pets (especially your beloved German Shorthaired Pointer) is that you must prepare him for the situations in which no one will be in the house. As such, we will get started with his personal area.

Setting Up His Personal Area

Allocate an area for your companion. Initially, you might want to confine him there, as to create the habit on your puppy, but don 't just trap him in a corner; you have to make this area his happy place, put his toys, food, water, and blanket there. This way, whenever he gets a little down he will return to his hideout to take a nap.

- I like versatility; so a dual, standing feeder (Amazon link at tiny.cc/mpub/dogs) was my choice. I recommend this setup over the traditional one because it allows for better digestion/eating, and avoids spilling altogether.

- Adding a nice dog bed would be a good idea; it might not look like it, but dogs like laying over comfortable surfaces just like we do! I got a plushy sofa-style bed for my dog (Amazon link at tiny.cc/mpub/dogs).

- I tossed a cozy, durable blanket (Amazon link at tiny.cc/mpub/dogs) on top to add more comfort; the fact that it covers the bed, preventing scratches, is a nice bonus.

Don't forget to add his potty area if you'll have it inside the house!

Prepare It For When You're Not Home

Be sure to leave him with enough food and water (and his toys!) before leaving, if you gave him a comfy little area to stay, he will faithfully wait for your return there.

This is a perfect moment to remind you about the importance of stocking up on treats. I like having two types of treats, one that is tasty, and excellent as a reward for training/good behavior, and another that is healthy, and good for digestion and dental health.

- Visit tiny.cc/mpub/dogs for the Amazon link to my recommended choice for the "training" treat
- There you'll also find my recommended choice healthy treats

Potty Training

Perhaps the most important type of training. Whether you choose to have it inside or outside the house, the steps remain the same: structure a schedule for your doggy and follow it. Generally speaking, you should take your dog to excrete at least twice per day, but 3 to 4 times per day would be ideal.

Just remember to be understanding if he does it inside the house, outside the allocated area; remember that your pet is only doing what it biologically needs to, and it doesn't understand this whole thing of potty train out of the box. Scold it with a firm "no" while looking at him directly in the eyes, and whenever he successfully does it in the correct place, reward it with some treats!

If you decided to go with the outside route, be sure to instill obedience when you take your dog out. If your objective is to have an obedient dog that you can take out without a leash, then you must make him follow you with commands. Check the next chapter for more information on this.

As a side note, try to avoid mistakes as much as possible, remember that, just like you have to go to the bathroom, and sometimes you feel you can't hold it any longer, your puppy feels the same; save him the mistakes by following the schedule, that way he will understand how and when to satisfy his needs without your input.

This pretty much covers house training for your puppy, with this information at hand and a few weeks of dedication, your rugs will feel way safer when your German Shorthaired Pointer is around.

Let's explore the fun part of training your dog, and that is... commands!

Part 4

Basic Commands

Before heading straight into crazy tricks and what-not, you need to train your dog with some basic commands; They're not only fun (and useful), but also essential for both the well-being, good behavior, and further training of your companion.

The following 5 commands are absolutely essential for the advanced commands. In fact, most advanced commands are actually a chain of basic commands ordered in a particular fashion!

"What are we doing, master?"

The commands in question are the following:

1. Sit
2. Lay
3. Come
4. Stay
5. Leave

1. Sit Command

This is the classic command, no dog-owner can say his furry friend is trained without having him do a mere "sit" first.

This command is also essential for the more advanced orders, and at first, teaching this trick to your friend shouldn't be hard at all! Although, if this is your first time training your dog, it will definitely take a bit of time.

① Hold a treat over your dog's head.   ② Move it straight back.   ③ Press his haunches while pulling up on the leash.

The steps to train your doggy are the following:

- Remember when I told you that you'd need a lot of treats for the training? Well, it is time to use them! Start by bringing a treat in your hand. Hold it close your dog to get his attention.

- Your dog will definitely turn its head to you expectantly, when you have his attention, slowly raise your hand; you will notice that your dog will track your hand with his eyes, and once your hand is up enough, he will sit in order to not strain his neck at a sharp 90 degree angle.

- Once the dog has sitting firmly on the ground, firmly say "sit" and then give it the treat, proceed to praise him for being

18

the best dog around!

- Once he sits, congratulations! You're well on your way to training him to sit. Firmly say "sit" when he is sitting, and proceed to give him the treat and some praise, this part is important because your dog will associate having a treat and praise with the act of "sitting".

- *Tip*: If your dog is not sitting reflexively, you can press his haunches while pulling up on the leash to help him into the position. Don't abuse this though!

These three steps are pretty basic and straightforward, be sure to repeat them several times per day, about 3 per day would be alright. Don't overdo the training! It's not really going to take you anywhere until the command is locked in.

After a week or two, you should notice that your dog will follow your order without a treat.

It is important to slowly take off the treats as well, during the training, after some effective days of sitting for treats, you should cut the treats, in order to have him follow you without them.

Besides being a supportive command for the advanced sequences, the "sit" command is super important, you can calm your canine when you're eating dinner or having some guests over, or maybe you're going to handle something dangerous like boiling water and you'd prefer if your dog stayed put in a corner.

You're doing fine buddy!

2. Lay Command

German Shorthaired Pointers are somewhat submissive, so training one to lay down shouldn't be too tricky. Keeping your dog happy and relaxed will definitely make things easier, otherwise, he might feel hesitant to lay at first.

Teach Your Dog to Lie Down

Step 1
Step 2
Step 3
Step 4

The steps to train your doggy are the following:

- Start by bringing a treat in your hand. Hold it close your dog to get his attention.

- Clench your fist, hiding the treat within, and slowly move it to the ground level.

Your furry friend will most likely stretch in the floor to sniff the treat.

- If he didn't stretch immediately, just move your hand forward, between his forelegs, and then back, away from him. This way he will track your hand with his head back, and then he will stretch to reach your fist when you move it away.

- Once he lays, congratulations! You're well on your way to training him to lay. Firmly say "lay" when he is laying on the ground, and proceed to give him the treat and some praise, this part is important because your dog will associate having a treat and praise with the act of "laying".

Do you see the trick already? Your dog will do things because he wants the reward, that being a tasty treat and some loving praise. This is how the training of dog goes, it is a matter of giving the right signals, rewarding, and praising your dog.

These steps are pretty easy and straightforward like the previous steps for training the "sit" command, but they shouldn't be repeated as much per day.

If your dog doesn't complete the

requirements (if he doesn't stretch completely or if he lunges to take the treat) you need to discourage that attitude by firmly saying "no" and removing your hand (and the treat) from the ground. It is of utmost importance that you don't give him the treat, as this will make your dog think about what he did to not receive the treat.

You have to instill obedience in your companion, so train him to follow the pattern of "do X to receive treat". It is the best thing you can do.

I recommend you thoroughly exercise both the "sit" and "lay" commands with your dog before going for the next commands, as these two will be absolutely necessary for the next sequences.

Excellent! Don't feel frustrated if your

German Shorthaired Pointer is being a bit stubborn for this one, just keep trying.

3. Come Command

The most useful command you can teach to your dog, bar none. Whenever your dog breaks out of the leash for any reason (It is not always your/his fault, entropy gets us eventually) you won't have to chase him (a dog running at 40 km/h) any longer!

But in the event your dog decides to start rushing directly into a roadway, you will have the ability to save him from doing that.

Teach Your Dog to Come

The steps to train your doggy are the following:

- Hopefully, you've got a long leash. You will need it! Put the leash on his collar and then order your German Shorthaired Pointer to sit, do so until he stays without following you.

- Make some distance with the dog, but not too much or he might stand up on his own accord to follow you.

- Swiftly tug the leash in your direction. If

your dog begins his walk toward you, congratulations! You're well on your way to training your dog to come over. Proceed to give him a treat and his much deserved praise.

This sequence isn't complex or anything, so be sure to repeat it about 2 or 3 times per day. As you progress the training, start making more distance between you and your dog, and then start doing it without the leash.

When everything is done, he will likely follow you without treats in the way!

Like the fastest steed, this recall command will bring back your companion at full speed!

4. Stay Command

This command will require your dog to sit, just like the "come" command, and its purpose is suiting your dog to patience and obedience because if you tell your dog to sit he might decide to stand up and not obey further "sit" commands.

Training the "stay" command will help you maintain your dog at a distance for a longer time than a mere "sit".

The steps to train your doggy are the following:

- Get your dog in a particular spot every time you get to train the command to be sure to bring him over to the same spot.

- Put your dog in "sit" in the designated spot, then open your palm in front of his face and firmly say "stay".

- Make some distance between you and the dog, not too far initially as he might stand up. Set a time goal; keep it short at first.

- If your dog stays put for at least the time goal you set, congratulations! Your dog is becoming more patient, give him a treat, proceed to praise him.

Repeat this sequence at least 3 times per day, but consider making it like sessions where you repeat the exercise 3 times in a row. As your dog understands the pattern, increase both the time goal and the distance.

It is important to discourage his impatience whenever he gets up without you telling him to do so, or when he does it too quickly, don't give him a treat and firmly say "no".

This way he will associate any directed "no" as a call to reflection.

This command will prove particularly useful when your dog is acting more hyperactive than usual, it should make him freeze like a statue until you call him!

Well... not so literally buddy!

5. Leave Command

The "leave" command is mainly used for telling your dog to either stop grabbing things he shouldn't or to make sure he doesn't try to eat anything dangerous. So it might be a potential life saver! It may prove tricky to teach, however.

The steps to train your doggy are the following 2 sequences:

Sequence I

- Bring two treats, one in each hand, and show them to your dog to get his attention.

- Clench your fist with the treat within with one hand, and bring that hand to your dog's face and say "leave", he will bark, sniff, lick and generally anything to get the treat inside, but you will ignore it.

- Once he stops trying to get the treat from your hand, and even better if he backs away, you will give him the treat from the other hand.

The purpose of this sequence is to instill the concept of not trying to get something that is considered wrong in order to get the "right" treat.

Sequence II

- Bring two treats, one that is considered "right" and one that is considered "wrong". Put the "wrong" treat on the ground and say "leave".

- Once he ignores the treat and looks at you, you give him the "right" treat, along praising of course.

The training process involves increasing the difficulty of sequence II by making more distance from the treat, up to the point you're standing several inches away from the treat. This will require several repetitions per week, and much patience as well.

This command might not be useful at the time, but it will instill the much-needed obedience your dog needs for advanced commands and overall discipline.

Ready for duty I see?

Part 5

Advanced Commands

Now, get ready to teach your German Shorthaired Pointer a few advanced tricks, with a little patience and effort, you will have a professional German Shorthaired Pointer!

We will be covering the following tricks for your canine:

1. Go to commands.
2. Roll
3. Beg
4. Heel

Eager to go, pal?

Go To Commands

Places

First, choose a place you want to use as a reference for the training, for the purposes of this guide, we will refer to "his blanket".

The steps to train your doggy are the following:

- Catch your dog's attention with a treat,

say "Go to" the blanket, and quickly place the treat on his blanket.

- Once he arrives at the blanket, he can have his treat, be sure to praise him for it!

This exercise won't take much to train, as it is actually pretty easy to perform.

Once the basic "go to part" is covered, proceed to the next level of the training.

- Say "Go to" the blanket, and when he arrives, tell him to "sit", "lay" or "stay" in the blanket.

- Set your time goal, and after he completes it, give him a treat, and proceed to praise him!

This command requires layering of other commands, and it requires patience above all because of that, so be ready to practice this a couple of times per day while you train your canine.

Generally, it proves to be very useful when you have a lot of things going on in the house and you need to make your dog settle in his personal area to avoid stress.

People

First, choose a helper for this command, typically you'd want to do it with the other members of the household, be sure to supply them with treats to give to your German Shorthaired Pointer!

It follows the same general line as the places commands, but this time it will require more input. For the purposes of this guide, I will use my name as a reference, David.

The steps to train your doggy are the following:

- Bring your dog and your helper to an area to train. Make sure to make a good distance between yourself and the helper.
- You will say "Go to" David to your dog and point at your helper. David should then call your dog by his name.

- Once your dog successfully reaches David, he should give him a treat, and proceed to praise him.

Be sure to practice this until your dog goes to your target without treats, and if you can, do it with a couple more of persons so that gets used to understanding names.

This covers the Go to commands, so now your furry friend should be able to navigate around the house at your instructions!

Roll Command

The roll command is perhaps one the most entertaining tricks you can teach to your companion, not really useful for anything (besides showing off to your friends) but it can be great fun with your furry friend.

Teach Your Dog to Roll Over

The steps to train your doggy are the following:

- Catch the attention of your dog with a

39

treat, and order him to "lay".

- Place the hand with the treat on his face, say "roll" and move it to one of the sides you want him to roll. He should lay on one of his sides, giving a tickle on the nether regions will cue him to do so if he doesn't.

- Now, move it further in the direction of the side you choose, in order for your dog to do the complete roll, maybe cue him what to do by moving his legs a few times, once he does it, give him the treat, and proceed to praise him! Your dog is well on his way to getting the favor from your friend.

The only trick for this command is being steady with the practice, repeat and repeat the sequence until your dog can perform this trick without needing your cues or treats!

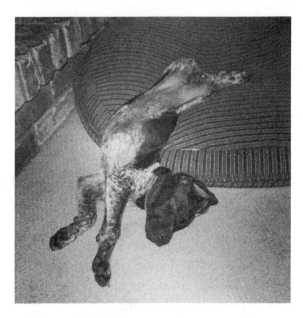

You're so great buddy! Now, let's impress our friends.

Beg

Another not-so-useful trick, but certainly an adorable one! Be sure to have tempered the obedience of your dog a high degree, as you probably don't like him begging at the dining table.

Teach Your Dog to Sit Pretty

The steps to train your doggy are the following:

- Catch the attention of your dog with a treat, and put him in "sit".

- Get the treat closer to his face, and then lift it up so that he has to raise its paws, keep moving back and forth until he rests on his haunches.

- Once he spends a couple of seconds in that position, give him a treat, and proceed to praise him for being so obedient and skilled.

This trick requires patience, as it often leads to the dog either sitting still or jumping, so iron out his flaws with a firm "no" and reward him for completing the goal!

Now the hard part is refusing to give him treats...

Heel

This command is great for walking out your dog in places that might have many distractions that could tempt him to break out of the leash. If you tempered his leash obedience, this trick should be very easy to teach!

The steps to train your doggy are the following:

- Have a walk with your dog, and bring a treat (or a few ones. Once your dog is relaxed and walking, shorten the leash a bit, call his name, say the command "heel" and show him the treat.

- Move the treat back while keeping the leash short until your dog is walking alongside your heels.

- Once he gets in your heel, while walking, give him the treat and proceed to praise him for being the best dog around!

It really helps to have a release word as well, I'd recommend saying "release" after loosening the leash so that your dog knows when he can return to his normal walking.

**You have mastered this training guide, buddy!
Isn't that great?**

Part 6

Troubleshooting Common Problems

You might bump into a brick wall during your training. Your dog may not be very inclined to follow some of your commands, or he may not perform them reliably. Fret not, however! I have some tips to help you in this scenario.

Not Answering To Your Call

So, your dog *sometimes* does come to you; when he does, he doesn't get close enough or quickly leaves. The reasons for this are many, but they often correlate "coming" with doing something they dislike, such as being put on the leash, taken inside, or being ordered to sit or stay.

As you can see, this is an unrewarded, low-value reward situation. They "earn" more by disregarding the order.

The solution?

Reward your dog. Whenever your dog actually comes after your call, use the opportunity to reward him with a toy, a game, or a treat. Then, try rewarding your dog scantly, about every five times he comes.

Pulling On the Leash

Your dog may have the habit of pulling and straining at the end of the leash to drag the person attached. This is concerning because the constant pulling can potentially cause harm to the dog's trachea and neck; not to mention that a stronger, more aggressive dog, could even trip the person. Without a gentle and tight control of your dog, the risks increase.

This occurs when dogs correlate "pulling on the leash" with their owners taking them where they want to get; the oppositional reflex of canines compels them to pull against pressure, as well.

The solution?

You need to modify your dog's behavior. Before, you might have given in to your dog's desire of getting to the place he wanted to get, but this contributes to the problem; instead, you will use your dog's reasoning to fix this problem.

All you have to do is the opposite of what you're used to: whenever your dog pulls on the leash, stop the walk. Once he slacks in the line, you can move again. This might require some time, but, unless your dog's behavior is the product of fear or aggression, it will eventually solidify into discipline.

Too Much Energy

Dealing with a dog whose only interest is releasing pent-up energy is hard. He won't pay attention to you, really. In this case, you do have to *give in* to your dog's desires.

The solution?

Exercise first, then discipline. Don't forget to add the affection at the end! Daily long walks that truly deplete the energy of your dog prior to the disciplinary training will go a long way.

Mixed Messages

Dogs are 100% about routines and consistency. If you're not being consistent with your training, your dog will tune out. Being "inconsistent" can take many forms:

- Maybe you're not training consistently; you take your time to train your dog today, but forget to do it the next week. This cannot happen, you must adhere to your schedule!

- You're telling your dog something is wrong, but then you're either allowing it or even rewarding it! This confuses him.

- Other family members enforce particular rules, which leads to further confusion for your dog.

Part 7

Recommended Products

A Dog Whistle

Whistles are constant, lack emotion, and carry their sound over large distances. This is an excellent tool for training! Basically, you can use it to teach all the commands to your dog, as well as helping him associate good things with the sound of the whistle to calm it! Visit tiny.cc/mpub/dogs for the Amazon link to my recommendation.

A Proper Feeder

Anything that makes the life of your dog better is worth a few bucks! More so when the product makes cleaning spilled liquids and food less of a chore. Visit tiny.cc/mpub/dogs for the Amazon link to my recommendation.

Tasty Treats

You're *really* going to need treats to effectively train your dog, there's no other way around it! Stocking on your dog's favorite treat is more important, so be sure to experiment with treats to find what your friend likes! Me? I use the ones called Zuke's Mini Naturals. Visit tiny.cc/mpub/dogs for the Amazon link.

Part 8

Conclusion

Whew! You and your German Shorthaired Pointer have come a long way, it seems like yesterday you were barely teaching him where to go to the bathroom, and now he is rolling over and heeling!

Thank you for taking the time to learn and train your German Shorthaired Pointer, your dog is a beautiful and loyal creature, be sure to remind him he truly is the best dog around.

Because every dog owner's dog is his best dog, it is the bond you create with your furry friend what matters the most!

I wish you well in your endeavors with this handsome dog, in fact, I motivate you to keep training your German Shorthaired Pointer with cools tricks, for example, you could teach him...

... how to bring flowers to your special someone, or even better! You could teach him...

... how to be your personal driver!

Either way, just remember to give him all the love he deserves! After all, you have an obedient dog that will never become a nuisance to your friends and family.

Farewell, valiant German Shorthaired Pointer trainer!

Sign up for Mobius Publishing updates and receive a **FREE BOOK** immediately! Visit tiny.cc/mpub to sign up.

You can also get information on upcoming book launches, free book promotions and much more!

Visit tiny.cc/mpub/rhodes where you can check out all my other books.

You can also reach me on Twitter at @MobiusBooks or on Facebook at @Mobius.Publishing.

Thank you and good luck,

Antony

Petcube Bites Wi-Fi
Pet Camera

With Treat Dispenser: 2-Way Audio, HD 1080p Video and Night Vision, For Dogs and Cats. Works With Amazon Alexa (As Seen On Ellen)

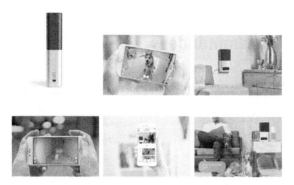

- WATCH: keep an eye on your pet and home when away with live 1080p HD video, 138 degree wide-angle view, night vision, 3x digital zoom.

- TREAT: fling treats to your pet remotely, from your phone. High capacity up to 2 lb container. 1- 5 treats may come out at one time depending on the treat size.

- TALK and HEAR: get your furry friend off the couch and hear what's going on with two-way audio and automatic sound-detection alerts.

- COMPATIBLE with ALEXA: All Petcube cameras work with Amazon Alexa (an optional add-on feature), so you can use voice commands to fling treats to your pet. Test your pet's agility by flinging treats varying distances, up to 6 feet

To Get It Now, Visit tiny.cc/mpub/dogs

More from Mobius Publishing

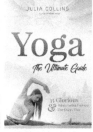

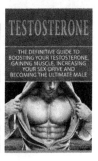

See our entire collection at
tiny.cc/mpub

DON'T FORGET! Get your bonus book: Backyard Chickens: The Ultimate Guide

As a special thank you to my readers, I am giving away free copies of *Backyard Chickens: The Ultimate Guide*. Enjoy eggs from your backyard while they're still warm! Reconnect with nature and your food by having your own chickens. It's easier than you think.

To get instant access to this book and more awesome resources, visit the link below:

Tiny.cc/mpub/free-gift-backyard-chickens

As an added bonus, subscribers will be given a chance to get exclusive sneak peaks of upcoming books and a chance to get free copies with no strings attached. Don't worry, we treat your e-mail with the respect it deserves. You won't get any spammy emails!!!

You might also be interested in...

Horse Training: The Complete Guide To Training the Best Horse Ever

The Essential Guide To Training Your Horse

"My colt is off to a great start because of this book."—Robert Costello, rancher

"Great advice, even for older horses! Easy to understand and implement."—Joyce

Ingham, riding enthusiast

This comprehensive, illustrated book draws upon Roger's years of horse training experience, including **over 12 years** with his own horse, *Toby*.

Horses are intelligent and quick learners, which makes them highly trainable. In fact, many consider them to be the smartest of all animals. This book contains the strategies you'll need to master the skill of horse training.

You Will Learn Exactly How To:

- **Understand** Your Horse
- **Connect** With Your Horse
- **No-fail techniques**
- **Cue** Your Horse
- Training Techniques
- General Horsemanship Tips
- Get Your Horse To Stop or Stand Still
- Deal With an **Anxious Horse**
- Riding Lessons

- Ride On Roads

And much, much more!

Includes Free Bonus Book: the Dutch Oven Cookbook!

Don't Miss Out, Get Your Copy Now!

Go to tiny.cc/mpub and search for *horse training* to see the entire book.

Preview of First Chapter:

Part 1

Understanding Your Horse

Horses are very intelligent, they're habit animals that respond well to regimentation, which means that, through perseverance, they will learn very quickly, as they react to repetition of routines and techniques.

Anyhow, they respond the best when they're connected with their rider, a horse must trust its rider in order to achieve anything in training, so developing a bond with your horse is first and foremost.

Just like us, they have personalities, and you must understand just how does your horse think, is it a timid horse that needs care and support? Is it a bold and rebellious hose that will need plenty of discipline and temperance? Or is it an obedient horse, ready to follow orders?

You must precise this information, before

you proceed to training.

Establishing a bond can be done in many ways, perhaps the most obvious one can be started with bodily contact, either by hands, whips, spurs or saddle, you need to understand what comforts and discomforts your horse.

With this information at hand, you just need to realize that a horse responds either seeking comfort, or avoiding discomfort, a rider that knows his horse will focus any training in making the situation comfortable for the horse.

If a horse is pressed against discomfort, its reaction will not be positive, and it may go from unresponsiveness to straight fright.

Horses are the speedy animals they are because they developed a strong natural instinct against danger, and in a scenario of

"Fight or Flight" they will more than likely pick flight, as such they evolved to be fast.

With that in mind, get to know hour horse, what comforts/discomforts it, and you'll have the vital information needed to train it!

To see the rest of *Horse Training: The Complete Guide To Training the Best Horse Ever* by Roger Cohen, search on Amazon or visit tiny.cc/mpub and search for *horse training*

Also consider:

The Dutch Oven Cookbook: 25 Handpicked, Delicious & Healthy Recipes For Every Day

"Best of all, my family ACTUALLY ATE them, and rated each dish a 'make this one again, please'."—Alfonzo

"My New Best Friend for Fuss-Free One-Pot Meals"—Tara

"Minimal prep time, recipes taste great!"— Lori

Your Dutch

Must-Have Oven

Cookbook For Your Dutch Oven!

Are You Looking For Delicious Easy To Make Dutch Oven Recipes That Save You Time and Money? This Book Could Be the Answer You're Looking For...

We all know that eating healthy is hard and cooking healthy food every day is even harder! Dutch ovens have taken off in popularity because they solve both issues at once. By making large healthy meals in one setting, you can have **nutritious and delicious meals that will last** for days. No more need to waste time cooking and cleaning every day!

This book is designed to empower you by providing **essential Dutch Oven cooking techniques** along with tasty recipes to help

69

you make delicious, nutritious meals.

You Get:

- How to choose your Dutch Oven
- How to care for your Dutch Oven
- How to clean Your Dutch Oven
- Other Useful Tips
- 25 Recipes For EVERY Meal - Breakfast, Lunch, Dinner and Dessert!

Learn How To Make These Awesome Recipes:

Breads

- Banana Bread
- Buttermilk Cornbread
- Monkey Bread
- Ginger Bread
- Mexican Corn Bread

Main Dishes

- Brown Sugar and Maple Steak Bites

- Vegetarian Chili
- Malatang
- Jambalaya
- Chicken Cordon Bleu Casserole
- Deep Dish Pizza
- Ratatouille
- German Sauerbraten
- Cheese Steak Soup
- Hawaiian meatballs

Vegetables

- Green Bean Casserole
- Vegetable Noodle Casserole
- Vegetable Parmesan
- Hot Pot Potatoes
- Zucchini Casserole

Desserts

- Orange Glaze Cake
- Skor Cake
- Peach Cobbler
- Raspberry Cobbler
- Chocolate Turtle Cake

And much, much more!

Don't Miss Out On These Delicious Recipes and Get Your Copy Today!

Go to tiny.cc/mpub and search for *dutch oven* to see the entire book.

Preview of First Chapter:

Part 1

Dutch Oven Care, Tips and Tricks

Choose Your Dutch Oven

The Dutch oven is well suited to almost any type of scenario, and as such, it has been adapted to suit all types of situations. If you plan to use it on camping trips with large groups, then you will be better off with a pot that's fourteen to sixteen inches in diameter. At ten to twelve inches, a family would find greater utility. Smaller sizes, as small as eight inches could also be found.

You may find Dutch ovens with bail handles made of heavy gauge wire to be exceedingly useful in almost any situation, especially if the bail handle is securely attached via tangs on the sides of the pot. Riveted tangs are to be avoided. If you are partial to a lighter pot that's easier to carry, then you may appreciate the aluminum varieties that can be found. Aluminum Dutch ovens do not require seasoning to ensure durability over time. Be advised however, that aluminum takes longer to heat and does not retain heat as long as the traditional cast iron versions. Cast iron varieties require care to provide long service to the Dutch oven purist. To keep the surfaces usable and intact, these pots must be seasoned and oiled. Users find that the longer heat retention and shorter heat-up time, render the time tested cast iron Dutch oven, a monolith in their cookware arsenal.

Care For Your Dutch Oven

Season your cast iron Dutch oven before use to ensure that it does not rust and that flavors from the foods you prepare are not absorbed into the porous cast iron. A Dutch oven that is properly seasoned will not require much cleaning and will get better with age.

Your cast iron adventure begins with the following steps:

1. Heat cookware and peel off label. If there are any irregularities in the underside of the metal such as burns or tarnishes - file them away.

2. Wash, rinse and dry with warm, soapy water.

3. Oil cookware. Spread an even film of oil over the entire surface of the pot. One tablespoon of oil should do.

4. Add more oil and heat. Add enough oil to cover the bottom of the utensil. Place in medium oven until oil is hot and thin (but not smoking!).

5. Lift Dutch oven off of heat and rotate so that oil re-coats the entire surface.

6. Add oil and heat at 200-250 for one hour. Leave utensil in oven over-night.

7. Wipe with a paper towel before use.

Clean Your Dutch Oven

Never use soap on cast iron cookware. Bring water to a boil and gently scrub with a sponge to remove stuck on food. Rinse and allow to air dry, then heat until the pot is warm to the touch. Apply a thin coat of oil to the inside of the oven and to the underside of the lid.

Other Useful Tips

Have on hand a good pair of gloves to assist with the handling of the Dutch oven. Leather gloves work well for this purpose and a pair of hot pot pliers can extend your capabilities in lifting the lid or grasping the handle in high heat situations. You may also want to keep a shovel handy if you plan to heat with coals.

A Quick Guide To Cooking

Techniques With the Dutch Oven

We're almost about to dive into the recipe section, just keep the following techniques in mind before you embark on your adventures with the Dutch oven.

To Roast

Place coals on the lid of the oven and beneath to oven at a 1 to 1 ratio. 20 coals should give about 500 degrees.

To Bake

Place more coals on top of the lid than underneath the oven at a ratio of 1 to 3 so that more heat comes from the top.

To Fry or Boil

All heat should come from beneath the pot.

To Stew or Simmer

Place almost all the coals beneath the pot at a ratio of 1 to 4

Now you're primed and ready to begin cooking!

To see the rest of *The Dutch Oven Cookbook: 25 Handpicked, Delicious & Healthy Recipes For Every Day* by Antony Rhodes, search on Amazon or visit tiny.cc/mpub and search for *dutch oven*

© Copyright 2018 by Antony Rhodes and Mobius Publishing. All rights reserved.

This document is geared towards providing exact and reliable information in regards to the topic and issue covered. The publication is sold with the idea that the publisher is not required to render accounting, officially permitted, or otherwise, qualified services. If advice is necessary, legal or professional, a practiced individual in the profession should be ordered.

- From a Declaration of Principles which was accepted and approved equally by a Committee of the American Bar Association and a Committee of Publishers and Associations.

The information provided herein is stated to be truthful and consistent, in that any liability, in terms of inattention or otherwise, by any usage or abuse of any policies, processes, or directions contained within is the solitary and utter responsibility of the recipient reader. Under no circumstances will any legal responsibility or blame be held against the publisher for any reparation, damages, or monetary loss due to the information herein, either directly or indirectly.

Respective authors own all copyrights not held by the publisher. The information herein is offered for informational purposes solely, and is universal as so. The presentation of the information is without contract or any type of guarantee assurance.

The trademarks that are used are without any consent, and the publication of the trademark is without permission or backing by the trademark owner. All trademarks and brands within this book are for clarifying purposes only and are the owned by the owners themselves, not affiliated with this document.

Made in the USA
Monee, IL
14 October 2022

15876691R00052